Visit **http://vocalimpactproductions.com/freegift/**
for your FREE 10-point checklist:
Do You Speak Like a Leader?

Maximize Your Leadership Influence

Command the Room,
Connect with Your Audience,
Close the Deal!

Laura Sicola, PhD

THiNKaha®

An Actionable Business Journal

E-mail: info@thinkaha.com
20660 Stevens Creek Blvd., Suite 210
Cupertino, CA 95014

Published by THiNKaha®
20660 Stevens Creek Blvd., Suite 210, Cupertino, CA 95014
http://thinkaha.com
E-mail: info@thinkaha.com

First Printing: April 2018
Hardcover ISBN: 978-1-61699-243-9   1-61699-243-3
Paperback ISBN: 978-1-61699-242-2   1-61699-242-5
eBook ISBN: 978-1-61699-241-5   1-61699-241-7
Place of Publication: Silicon Valley, California, USA
Paperback Library of Congress Number: 2017963541

Trademarks

Warning and Disclaimer

Dedication

To my husband, Larry, for supporting me in everything I do, and to my sons, Thomas and Dante—may they grow up with a leader's voice and a servant's heart.

Acknowledgement

First, special thanks to Mitchell Levy for inviting me to write this book and to Jenilee Maniti for being a great project manager along the way, both of whom helped me get it published in record time.

J.V. Crum III, my amazing business coach, has been a source of clarity, confidence, and continued growth, guiding key decisions and promoting consciousness in making the world a better place through business development.

Early inspiration came from the late Dr. Miwa Nishimura, my Japanese professor in college, who first said to me, "You should be a linguist," and the late Dr. Teresa Pica, my PhD advisor, who encouraged me to do interdisciplinary research that has had such an important influence in my work today. May their contributions and memories continue to inspire people.

I owe a debt of gratitude to Chris Caine, who gave me my first consulting opportunity and showed me that my work had widespread application, and to Grace Killelea, who first called my work in leadership and voice, "a game changer."

I am also grateful to my clients—past, present, and future—who continue to inspire me daily with their commitment to growth.

Last but not least, I am grateful to my family, especially my parents, Tom and Nadine, and my husband, Larry, who have always encouraged me to follow my dreams, and my sons, Thomas and Dante, who make me want to be a better person every day.

How to Read a THiNKaha® Book
A Note from the Publisher

The THiNKaha series is the CliffsNotes of the 21st century. The value of these books is that they are contextual in nature. Although the actual words won't change, their meaning will change every time you read one as your context will change. Experience your own "AHA!" moments ("AHAmessages™") with a THiNKaha book; AHAmessages are looked at as "actionable" moments—think of a specific project you're working on, an event, a sales deal, a personal issue, etc. and see how the AHAmessages in this book can inspire your own AHAmessages, something that you can specifically act on. Here's how to read one of these books and have it work for you:

1. Read a THiNKaha book (these slim and handy books should only take about 15–20 minutes of your time!) and write down one to three actionable items you thought of while reading it. Each journal-style THiNKaha book is equipped with space for you to write down your notes and thoughts underneath each AHAmessage.

2. Mark your calendar to re-read this book again in 30 days.

3. Repeat step #1 and write down one to three more AHAmessages that grab you this time. I guarantee that they will be different than the first time. BTW: this is also a great time to reflect on the actions taken from the last set of AHAmessages you wrote down.

After reading a THiNKaha book, writing down your AHAmessages, re-reading it, and writing down more AHAmessages, you'll begin to see how these books contextually apply to you. THiNKaha books advocate for continuous, lifelong learning. They will help you transform your ahas into actionable items with tangible results until you no longer have to say "AHA!" to these moments—they'll become part of your daily practice as you continue to grow and learn.

As The AHA Guy at THiNKaha, I definitely practice what I preach. I read 2-3 AHAbooks a month in addition to those that we publish and take away two to three different action items from each of them every time. Please e-mail me your AHAs today!

Mitchell Levy
publisher@thinkaha.com

THiNKaha®

Contents

Introduction

You want to be an effective leader, whether you're at the top already or aspire to be there some day. But one of the biggest obstacles is that to do so, you have to go beyond intelligence, knowledge, and skill.

One phrase I have heard all too often about people in leadership positions and high potentials alike is: "They are, by far, the most technically qualified for the role, *but*..." That "but" is the kiss of death. It is inevitably followed by a reference to deficient leadership communication skills. The inability to project confidence and executive presence. Rambling and boring presentations. Getting bogged down in excruciating detail nobody cares about. Being too confrontational or too non-confrontational. Being too tactical and not strategic. The list goes on and on.

Your ability to communicate clearly, diplomatically, relatably, authoritatively, and authentically plays just as big a role as your skill and experience in determining whether you successfully come across as a leader who is truly worth following. Because when you can check that box, that's when you *really* have influence.

But that kind of communication ability is more difficult than it sounds. It can't be done effectively and reliably through text messages and emoticons (despite what my teenage son would have you believe). Even face-to-face conversation, which offers far more context and opportunity for effective communication, can go south in a split second with an unconscious facial expression or unappreciated tone of voice.

Think about it: just about everyone has had an argument with someone in which one person said, "Why are you mad? What did I say?" and the other responded, "It's not what you said, it's how you said it." Of course, it's really the combination of the words you use (the "what you said") and your delivery (the "how you said it") that determines how your message lands. While this particular exchange tends to be more typical in personal relationships, this kind of miscommunication is just as prevalent in your professional life, even if it's not so bluntly addressed.

The problem occurs because most people are only clear on two out of three impressions: they know the impression they want to make, and they know the impression they *think* they're making as they speak, but more than likely, they have no idea what kind of impression they *actually* make.

That's where I come in: my job is to help you close that gap. First, by helping you identify your blind spots regarding how you actually come across and how it might detract from the impact you want to have. Then, by disentangling all the little communication cues that you don't even realize you're sending out, and seeing which ones are contributing to that (mis)impression. And finally and most importantly, by showing you how to drop those cues, habits, and behaviors that have been sabotaging your success and undermining your image, and replacing them with new cues, habits, and behaviors that will build the ideal image and reputation you want.

I challenge you to take the following 140 AHAmessages as an invitation. Let me be your guide. Read. Reflect. Record. Reflect some more. Have both the curiosity and courage to begin to explore and close your own gap. You don't just owe it to the people you lead— you owe it to yourself.

When you can close the gap, that's when ears, minds, and hearts start to open. That's when doors open. That's when you'll realize you've mastered the Three Cs and can:

Command the Room,
Connect with the Audience,
and
Close the Deal.

That is the power of influence.

Share the AHA messages from this book socially by going to
http://aha.pub/LeadershipInfluence.

Section I
Speech, Credibility, and Influence

Influence. It's the ultimate differentiator between a leader who can effectively lead an organization to turn an exciting vision into an even more exciting reality, and someone who can't. But how can you have the right kind of influence—the kind that inspires people and makes them want to be a part of whatever you are trying to create?

Hint: Influence starts with credibility, and your credibility is based how well you communicate. Every time you speak, whether on the phone, in a meeting, or when giving a formal presentation to major stakeholders, you either strengthen your image and reputation as a leader, or you undermine it.

Fundamentally, you must master the art of aligning your verbal, vocal and visual messaging. When they are aligned, that is the source of your power and influence. Not sure if you're in alignment when you speak? Turn the page to find out...

1

Leadership is an image. If people don't perceive you as a true leader, you're just the boss. #LeadershipImage @LauraSicola

_____

_____

_____

2

Watch @LauraSicola's TED talk!
"Want to sound like a leader?
Start by saying your name right."
http://aha.pub/LauraSicolaTEDtalk

_____

_____

_____

3

You don't just want to have a leadership
role; you need to be a master influencer.
#CommunicationIsKey @LauraSicola

_____

_____

_____

4

Don't just speak. You have to
#MakeYourWordsMatter. All of them.
#SpeakingToInfluence @LauraSicola

_____

_____

_____

5

True power and influence is when you get people to see that you're a leader they genuinely want to follow. #LeadershipImage @LauraSicola

_____

_____

_____

6

Inspiration is the catalyst for action. Be a catalyst. #InspireAndBeInspired #Influence @LauraSicola

_____

_____

_____

7

People have to buy into you first before they buy into your product, service, or idea. #Credibility @LauraSicola

_____

_____

_____

8

People will fixate on how you communicate, the most powerful factor that influences their gut-level evaluation of you.
@LauraSicola

_____

_____

_____

9

Don't just be a figurehead, #BeAVisionary.
How? Learn how to communicate your
vision to others. #LeadershipVision
@LauraSicola

_____

_____

_____

10

Influence is about getting people on board
with your vision and inspiring people to act
on it. #Inspiration #Leadership
@LauraSicola

_____

_____

_____

11

Think you don't do much public speaking?
#PublicSpeaking is any time you're talking
to someone other than yourself.
@LauraSicola

_____

_____

_____

12

To get people to shift their thinking and behavior, start with coming across as being credible. #HaveCredibility @LauraSicola

_____

_____

_____

13

Never speak without first identifying the purpose, goal, or objective you want to accomplish. #SpeakToLead #GetToYes @LauraSicola

_____

_____

_____

14

Ask yourself: What outcome do you want to see as a result of this conversation? Then, stay on course. #LeadershipCommunication @LauraSicola

_____

_____

_____

15

Your #Reputation is what happens in the moments when you're not actively trying to build it. #LeadershipImage @LauraSicola

_____

_____

_____

16

The way you speak will either strengthen your image or undermine it. Take control now. @LauraSicola
http://vocalimpactproductions.com

_____

_____

_____

17

It's not just how you can speak when necessary; your leadership image is based on how you usually speak. #LeadershipImage @LauraSicola

_____

_____

_____

18

Do you think you're an interesting speaker? Ask five of your friends and colleagues for honest feedback. #CommunicationIsKey @LauraSicola

_____

_____

_____

19

A captive audience is forced to listen against their will. A #captivated audience is engrossed. Which kind do you create? #Influence @LauraSicola

_____

_____

_____

20

How can you ensure that your next audience is #Captivated when you speak? That's your responsibility. Make a plan. #Influence @LauraSicola

_____

_____

_____

21

Video record yourself. It helps you see the impression you actually make in comparison to the impression you want to make. Take notes! #Truth @LauraSicola

_____

_____

_____

22

The irony: "Soft skills" can be HARD to master. Don't take them for granted! They are not optional ingredients in the recipe for success. #LeadershipCommunication. @LauraSicola

_____

_____

_____

23

#Credibility and trust are based on
how you communicate. Both how
you talk and how you listen matter.
#LeadershipCommunication. @LauraSicola

_____

_____

_____

24

#Credibility is founded on Verbal, Vocal, and Visual #ChannelsOfCommunication relaying the same message at the same time. @LauraSicola

_____

_____

_____

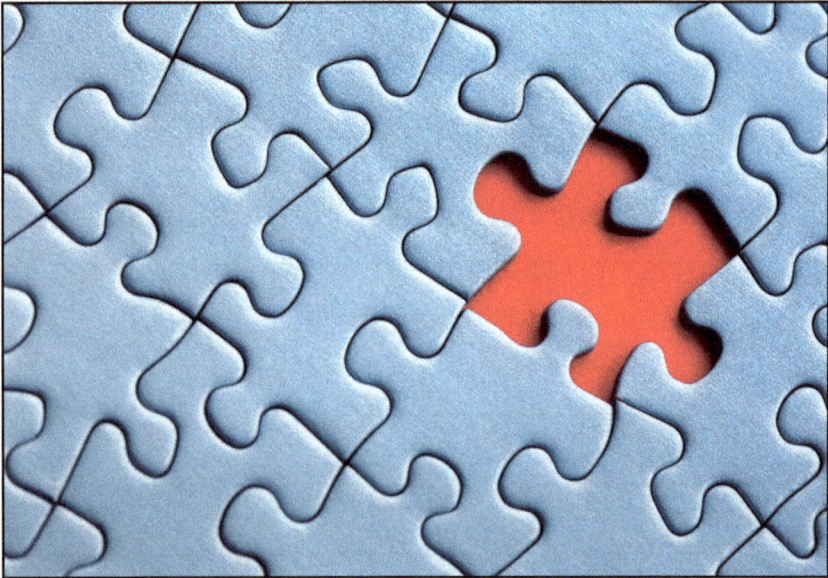

Share the AHA messages from this book socially by going to
http://aha.pub/LeadershipInfluence.

Section II
Why Expertise Is Not Enough

Being seen as a true leader takes so much more than having technical expertise. Your ability to clearly share that expertise with others, no matter who they are, is at the heart of the art of persuasion and influence.

Crucial to mastering these skills is the willingness and ability to learn and grow. Have you felt stagnant? That changes today. As you read, be open to exploring how to build the necessary communication skills to make the leap from just being "smart" or "great at your job," to being seen as a leader worth following, i.e. a master of influence.

25

Do you just want to be the best at your job, or do you want to be the best of the best at the top? #LeadershipCommunication @LauraSicola

_____

_____

_____

26

What will get you to the top is your ability to convey your vision clearly to key players, whether or not they share your expertise. #Influence @LauraSicola

_____

_____

_____

27

Show that your vision is even greater than your expertise. How? Share it in a way that gets through to ears, minds, and hearts.
@LauraSicola

_____

_____

_____

28

If you're seen as a leader, people will do
what you need them to do because they
want to, not because they have to.
#Influence @LauraSicola

29

If all you have is your technical expertise,
you're only proving that you should stay
exactly where you are. #Influence
@LauraSicola

30

It's great to be known for something, but don't you want to be known for more than just "something"? #Legacy #Reputation @LauraSicola

_____

_____

_____

31

Marshall Goldsmith: "What got you here won't get you there." https://amazon.com/ What-Got-Here-Wont-There/dp/0739342231 What got you here: Technical expertise. What will get you there: #CommunicationSkills. @LauraSicola

_____

_____

_____

32

To be a leader, you need to learn and grow. The day you're done learning is the day you're done. #LeadershipStartsWithLearning @LauraSicola

_____

_____

_____

33

If you only strive to improve your technical skills, you're only growing in one dimension. #Leadership is 3D. @LauraSicola

_____

_____

_____

34

Mentor others to be great at YOUR job. If you're irreplaceable in that role, you won't be allowed to move up! #RiseToTheTop @LauraSicola

_____

_____

_____

35

To become the person you want to be, you have to know the weaknesses keeping you from achieving it. #CommunicationIsKey #SelfAwareness @LauraSicola

---

36

You need to know if you are just okay at doing something, but not great at it. Improvement starts with #SelfAwareness. @LauraSicola

---

37

Do you recognize the difference
between getting by and excelling?
Getting by = Getting a C+. Excelling = A+.
#StriveForExcellence
@LauraSicola

_____

_____

_____

38

Have the courage to
#StepOutOfYourComfortZone to
see if your communication style is
effective or not in different contexts.
#EffectiveCommunication @LauraSicola

_____

_____

_____

39

Launch yourself out of your comfort zone --
no seatbelts. That's when massive, positive
change can occur. #SelfImprovement
@LauraSicola

_____

_____

_____

40

Record yourself to see what you did or didn't do well, so you can learn from it and knock it out of the park next time. Prepare to surprise yourself! #SelfAwareness #SelfImprovement @LauraSicola

_____

_____

_____

41

In order to grow, you have to be willing to practice something that feels awkward at first until it becomes second nature. #PracticeMakesPerfect @LauraSicola

_____

_____

_____

42

Everyone deals with a learning curve. "Fake it till you become it." --Amy Cuddy via @LauraSicola https://ted.com/talks/amy_ cuddy_your_body_language_shapes_who_ you_are #StriveForExcellence

_____

_____

_____

43

Think making videos isn't necessary because you already know your strengths and weaknesses? Trust me: take the challenge! #SelfAwareness @LauraSicola

_____

_____

_____

44

Many people are afraid to watch themselves on video because they fear it will be worse than it really is. Be curious: Watch! @LauraSicola

---

45

If you want to advance but your ego is afraid to learn the truth, you're suppressing any true potential for growth. @LauraSicola

---

46

Humiliation destroys dignity, but humility restores it. Ego gets in the way. Watch with humility. #LeadershipDevelopment #PowerOfHumility @LauraSicola

_____

_____

_____

47

If you are overly sensitive to constructive and even negative feedback, you'll never improve and grow. #Leadership #PowerOfHumility @LauraSicola

---

48

Effective leaders need to be confident enough to hear all feedback graciously and learn from it. #Leadership @LauraSicola

---

49

If you've tried to avoid learning "soft skills" for years, it will come back to bite you when you want to get to the top.
@LauraSicola

_____

_____

_____

50

You need to master the soft skills, just like you've mastered your technical area of expertise. #LeadershipCommunication
@LauraSicola

_____

_____

_____

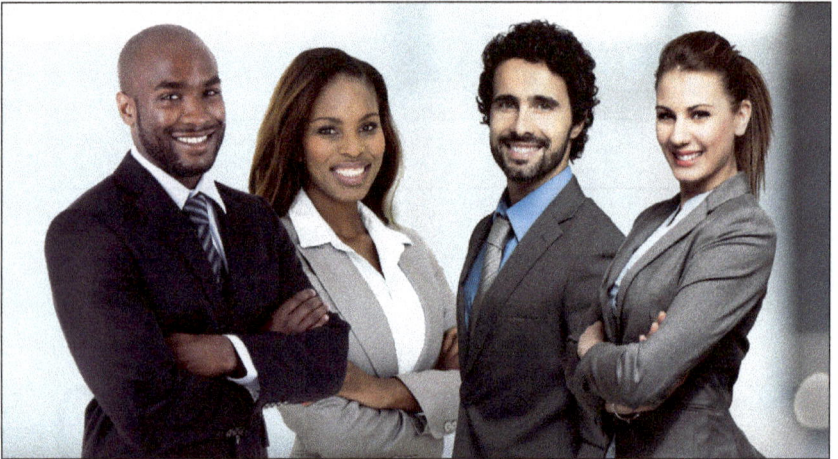

Share the AHA messages from this book socially by going to
http://aha.pub/LeadershipInfluence.

Section III
#ExecutivePresence

Have you ever met someone who had the ability to speak in a way that commanded your full attention? Who had this incredible magnetism and credibility when they spoke, so you were completely engrossed in what they were saying, whether during a formal speech or a one-on-one conversation? This is called "vocal executive presence."

What is executive presence in general? It's a combination of expertise, communication skills, decision-making and execution skills, and even your appearance, that allows you to think, speak, act, and look like a leader. Vocal executive presence drives it all home.

How do leaders develop executive presence overall and vocal executive presence specifically? Conscious awareness and practice are critical. But the goal is to master the Three Cs: Command the room, Connect with the audience, and Close the deal. That's influence from start to finish.

51

#ExecutivePresence = demonstrating integrity, expertise, authority, authenticity, and vulnerability. #LeadershipCommunication @LauraSicola

_____

_____

_____

52

#ExecutivePresence allows people to believe that you are THE authority when you stand up and speak in front of others.
@LauraSicola

_____

_____

_____

53

#ExecutivePresence requires good communication skills. It's essential to be both a good listener AND a good speaker. Are you? Who ELSE thinks so?
@LauraSicola

_____

_____

_____

54

If you want to succeed at the top, you need to have #ExecutivePresence and be able to #SpeakLikeALeader. #CommandTheRoom @LauraSicola

_____

_____

_____

55

Master the 3 Cs of influence: #CommandTheRoom, #ConnectWithTheAudience, and #CloseTheDeal. @LauraSicola

_____

_____

_____

56

Think about how you lead and present. Are you just getting by, or are you knocking it out of the park? #PushForExcellence @LauraSicola

_____

_____

_____

57

There's a difference between having
an audience that is truly *captivated* vs.
simply held *captive*. Which kind is yours?
#Captivate @LauraSicola

_____

_____

_____

58

You know you could be a better
communicator, but will your ego get
in the way of becoming truly great?
#PowerOfHumility @LauraSicola

_____

_____

_____

59

There's a difference between inherently
commanding respect and verbally
demanding respect. Which do you do?
#CommandNotDemand @LauraSicola

_____

_____

60

Commanding the room is having a presence that lets people know that in that moment, you're the authority. #CommandTheRoom @LauraSicola

_____

_____

_____

61

Commanding respect is something about the way you lead that makes people inherently respect you. #CommandNotDemand @LauraSicola

_____

_____

_____

62

Connecting with the audience is how you make listeners feel like you're speaking to them personally. #BeRelatable @LauraSicola

_____

_____

_____

63

Anybody who will listen to what you say, in any context, is your audience. Focus on their needs and connect with them. @LauraSicola

_____

_____

_____

64

If you connect with the audience, you can inspire them to change the way they think and act. #SpeakToInspire @LauraSicola

_____

_____

_____

65

You need to be able to connect with your audience regardless of their industry, role, age, ethnicity, and gender. #SpeakToInspire @LauraSicola

_____

_____

_____

66

If you have great content but lousy delivery, your message gets washed away and no one will ever internalize it. #CharismaticLeadership @LauraSicola

---

67

To #CloseTheDeal means getting to a "yes" and achieving your objective for the conversation or presentation. @LauraSicola

68

Your #SpeechRepertoire is a combo of what you say, how you sound, and how you look when saying it. It differs in each context. Develop your speech repertoire.
@LauraSicola

_____

_____

_____

69

The Three #ChannelsOfCommunication
are the Verbal, Vocal, and Visual channels.
They must work together for maximum
#Influence. @LauraSicola

_____

_____

_____

70

When #ChannelsOfCommunication are not aligned, the listener gets distracted. They miss your core message; you miss your chance. @LauraSicola

_____

_____

_____

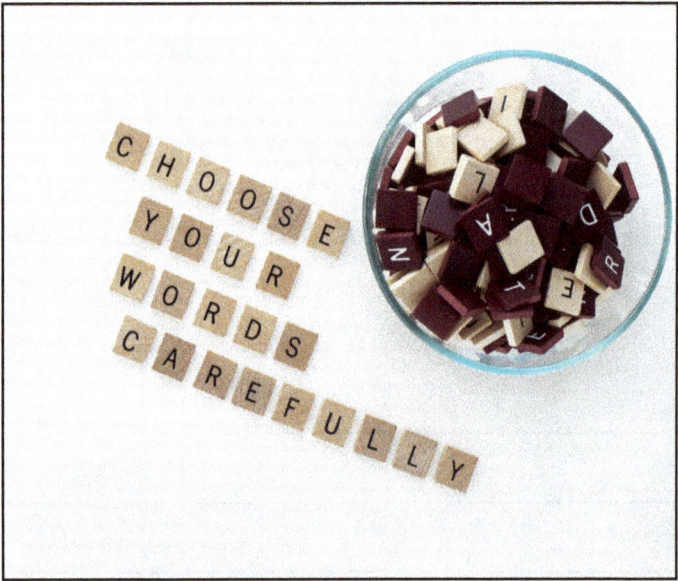

Share the AHA messages from this book socially by going to
http://aha.pub/LeadershipInfluence.

Section IV
Verbal: The Power of Words

Words matter, period. They are the structural "bones" of your message. If you want to have a positive influence, your word choice needs to be crystal clear. But it's not just about the individual words themselves; the overall content you choose to include or omit can be the difference between whether the response you get is "Oh," or "OH!"

How do you organize your information? Do you use lots of technical words (jargon) and details? Maybe too much or not enough? Do you tell stories and use examples to bring your data to life? If you don't have the right balance, you're missing the mark.

The challenge is that from situation to situation, the same examples, details, and word choices may or may not have the same impact, depending on who your audience is. Start with asking yourself, "What do these people need to know, and why?"

71

The Verbal channel is the actual words
you choose. Are they technical, accurate,
detailed, diplomatic, formal, other?
@LauraSicola

_____

_____

_____

72

Content has meat, and gravy: Gravy makes
your message enjoyable, but without
enough meat, it lacks substance and doesn't
satisfy. @LauraSicola

_____

_____

_____

73

If you're a charismatic speaker but lack real or comprehensible content, it's only a matter of time before they see through you. #Credibility @LauraSicola

_____

_____

_____

74

Great delivery of weak content is like putting #LipstickOnAPig: It might be entertaining, but it's still a pig. @LauraSicola

_____

_____

_____

75

When presenting, you have to provide value, regardless of time limits. You always have enough time to #GetToThePoint @LauraSicola

_____

_____

_____

76

The difference between relevant and essential info is the difference between whether they get it or wait for you to get there. #GetToThePoint @LauraSicola

_____

_____

_____

77

Which details are essential? If someone asks, "So what?" can you show why it matters for them? If so, it's essential. If you can't, it's not. #Connect @LauraSicola

_____

_____

_____

78

When you compare your "so what" answers, you'll see which have the biggest exclamation points. Make those your priority. #ExecutivePresence @LauraSicola

_____

_____

_____

79

The higher you go up the corporate ladder, the fewer details most people want to hear. #GetToThePoint #ManagingUp @LauraSicola

_____

_____

_____

80

How do you engage your audience through the nature of your content? How do you know they're engaged? #Connect @LauraSicola

_____

_____

_____

81

Hone your content (vocabulary, stories, details, etc.) based on who your audience is and what they came for. #Connect #ExecutivePresence @LauraSicola

_____

_____

_____

82

The stories you tell and the supporting details you provide your audience will make them say, "Oh, I get it!" #Connect #Influence @LauraSicola

_____

_____

_____

83

Situational context will dictate the majority of what info you should and should not include in your message. #LeadershipCommunication @LauraSicola

_____

_____

_____

84

People are not inspired by facts; people
are inspired by stories they can relate to.
#LeadershipCommunication @LauraSicola

_____

_____

_____

85

You can't just recite the data on a spreadsheet/slide; you have to tell the story of the data in order to bring it to life. @LauraSicola

_____

_____

_____

86

In a story, you have to prioritize the right details. Make sure your audience understands the most critical factors first. #GetToThePoint @LauraSicola

_____

_____

_____

87

People want you to #GetToThePoint;
don't overwhelm them with tons of detail.
Understand how much they need and want.
@LauraSicola

_____

_____

_____

88

Fillers like, "I mean," "You know," or "Um," will only fill the listener's head with, "No." #LeadershipCommunication #SpeakWithAuthority @LauraSicola

---

89

Do you use educated-sounding fillers like "Actually," "Basically," or "Really" instead of "um"? It's not better. #CommandTheRoom @LauraSicola

---

90

Fillers undermine your credibility because they make it sound like you aren't sure or don't believe what you're saying.
@LauraSicola

_____

_____

_____

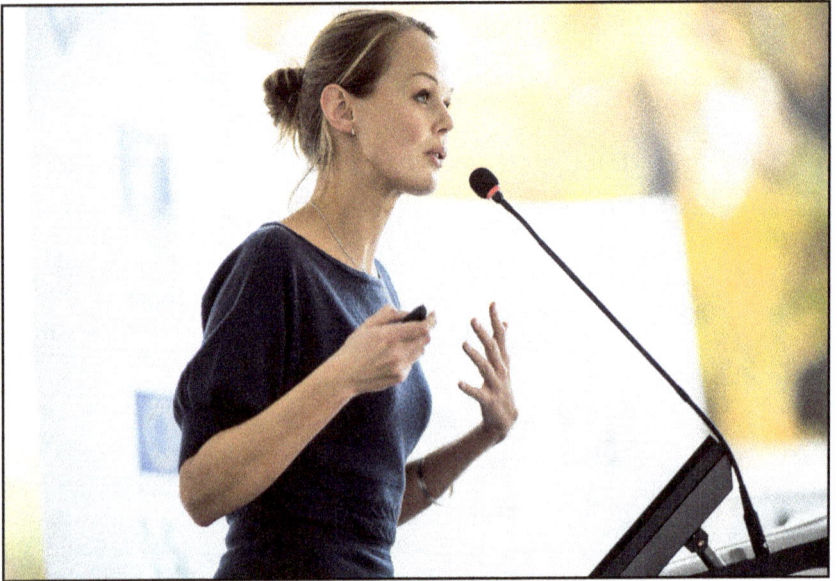

Share the AHA messages from this book socially by going to
http://aha.pub/LeadershipInfluence.

Section V
Vocal: The Sound of Leadership

Just like content, how you sound when you speak can have a powerful effect on the way your message lands. The tiny details of how you use your voice can either compel your audience to eagerly listen for more, or make them completely tune out. Which impact do you want to have?

You only have one voice... but there are infinite ways you can use it to create the meaning you want people to hear in your message. How you use (or misuse) your voice is even more important than your words when it comes to conveying to the listener what you meant by what you said. Are you even aware of what your voice makes people believe about your meaning?

Take a look (and listen); you may just be surprised by what you hear.

91

The vocal channel is the sound of your voice: the sound of the words as they come out of your mouth. #LeadershipVoice @LauraSicola

_____

_____

_____

92

Subconsciously, people want the messenger's voice to fit the nature of the message. #LeadershipCommunication @LauraSicola

_____

_____

_____

93

Good #VocalCommunication takes your words from black-and-white text and paints them in technicolor. @LauraSicola

_____

_____

_____

94

The content tells people what you think, but the delivery lets them know how you feel about what you're saying. @LauraSicola

_____

_____

_____

95

The voice has both cognitive and emotional effects on listeners. Learn to use that power to your benefit. #VocalCommunication @LauraSicola

_____

_____

_____

96

People don't understand you fully and completely unless you speak in a way that captivates. #LeadershipCommunication @LauraSicola

_____

_____

_____

97

The smallest details of how you sound
when you speak have huge influence
and impact on how your words land.
#LeadershipVoice @LauraSicola

_____

_____

_____

98

The way you sound will determine
whether your audience hears
what you say AND what you mean.
#SpeakToInfluence @LauraSicola

_____

_____

_____

99

Example: Vocal delivery lets you know if someone is being sincere or sarcastic, even though both ways look the same on paper. #VocalImpact @LauraSicola

_____

_____

_____

100

Try it: Say, "Nice shirt," like you mean it.
Now say it again as if the shirt is hideous.
Of course you hear the difference.
#VocalImpact @LauraSicola

_____

_____

_____

101

For people to hear your underlying message, don't let your voice and body language distract them. #VocalAlignment @LauraSicola

---

102

Factors in good #VocalCommunication: speed, volume, intonation, tonality, rhythm, use of pauses, breath support, and more. #VocalImpact @LauraSicola

---

103

Fast talker? PAUSE in between points to let people's brains catch up with their ears. It makes a difference! #VocalCommunication #VocalImpact @LauraSicola

_____

_____

_____

104

Tonality is key to conveying how important your message is and which PARTS of your message are MOST important. #VocalImpact @LauraSicola http://vocalimpactproductions.com/capturing-your-confidence-on-camera

_____

_____

105

Draw people's attention to key words using vocal emphasis. #EffectiveCommunication @LauraSicola

_____

_____

_____

106

#EffectiveSpeakers emphasize the most important words with higher pitch and greater length. #LeadershipCommunication @LauraSicola

_____

_____

_____

107

Up-speak(?)/up-talk(?) is that annoying habit(?) that sounds like someone is constantly inflecting "Right?" or "Okay?" You know? #NoUpTalk @LauraSicola

_____

_____

_____

108

When speaking, don't end every phrase with rising question-like pitch. It sounds like you constantly need validation. #NoUptalk @LauraSicola

---

109

If you sound like you constantly seek validation, you won't sound like you are ready to lead. #LeadershipCommunication @LauraSicola

---

110

When making a statement, allow your voice to declare it with falling pitch at the end of your sentence. #SpeakLikeALeader @LauraSicola

_____

_____

_____

Share the AHA messages from this book socially by going to
http://aha.pub/LeadershipInfluence.

Section VI
Visual: The Look of a Leader

If you want to be seen as a leader, you need to look the part. People base their first impressions on how you look before even hearing you speak. Your body language tells its own story that will either reinforce or undermine their belief in what your words say, because it telegraphs how you feel; it expresses how you feel about what you're saying and how much you believe your own words. The way you are dressed also tells the listener how you feel about them and about yourself. It's the wrapping paper on your gift to them. So, are you going to use a beautiful, shiny roll of paper, or an old newspaper?

But here's the thing—this also changes from situation to situation, so be ready to adjust your clothes and your mannerisms alike, in order to ensure that you exude the qualities they need to see in someone who is delivering your message. As they say, first impressions are lasting impressions, so what is yours?

111

The visual channel is how you look when you speak. What do people see, and does it match your words and voice? #LeadershipImage @LauraSicola

_____

_____

_____

112

Make a video of yourself talking. Now watch it on MUTE. What signals are you sending? #LeadershipCommunciation @LauraSicola

_____

_____

_____

113

You can't deny what you see: The video camera doesn't lie. (But it does add 10 pounds...) #PhysicalCommunication @LauraSicola

_____

_____

_____

114

The visual is the first filter through which people interpret what they think you meant and who they think you are. @LauraSicola

_____

_____

_____

115

Factors in good #PhysicalCommunication include body language, facial expression, attire, hair and grooming, posture, and more. @LauraSicola

_____

_____

_____

116

Use the acronym P.E.G.S. (Posture, Eye contact, Gestures, Smile) as a mental checklist for #PhysicalCommunication. @LauraSicola

_____

_____

_____

117

For your audience to hear your underlying message, don't distract them with confusing visual cues. Help them focus on the gift inside, not the wrapping paper. #PhysicalCommunication @LauraSicola

_____

_____

_____

118

A speaker needs to dress and speak appropriately for the situation so the audience listens with full attention. @LauraSicola #CommandTheRoom

_____

_____

_____

119

There's a time and a place to wear a T-shirt and jeans, and a time and place to wear a suit. Both matter. Know the difference. #CommandTheRoom @LauraSicola

_____

_____

_____

120

You can't always wear the same outfit for every occasion. The same goes for your speaking style. #LeadershipCommunication @LauraSicola

_____

_____

_____

121

Physical cues let people know how they should feel about what you're saying based on how it looks like YOU feel about it. #LeadershipCommunication @LauraSicola

_____

_____

_____

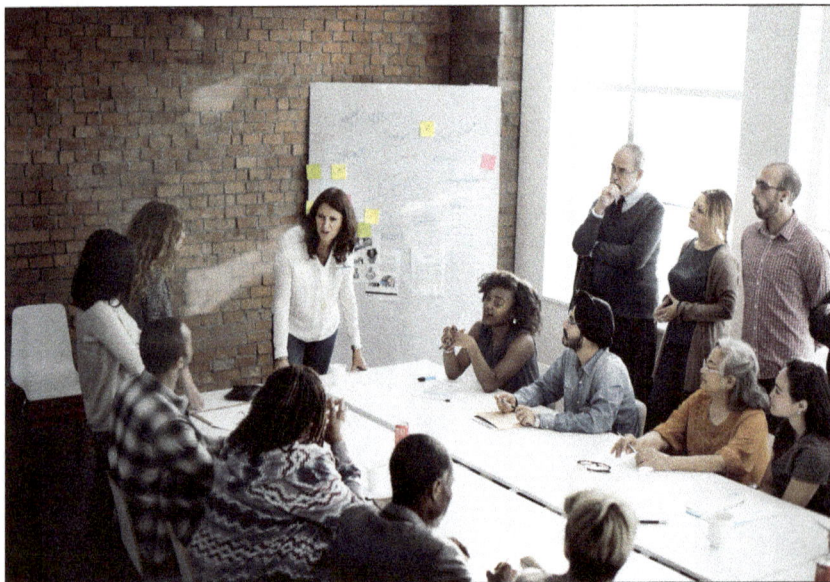

Share the AHA messages from this book socially by going to
http://aha.pub/LeadershipInfluence.

Section VII
Authenticity and Impact:
Connecting with Your Audience

Whomever you're talking to—whether it's just one person or an entire room of people—you need to be able to connect with them despite differences. How do you connect with your audience? It starts by knowing who they are.

The beauty is that you can adjust your speech style without sacrificing your identity. It's not about faking it or being someone you're not. The goal is simply be your authentic self, while still minimizing anything you do that might distract them from hearing the core of your message. If you can learn to comfortably do that, you'll discover first hand what true influence feels like.

122

If you want to be an effective CEO, you have to be able to manage cross-functional, multicultural and international teams. To do that, you have to understand them first. #LeadershipCommunication @LauraSicola

_____

_____

_____

123

Do you know who your audience is, what they want, and how to give it to them? #LeadershipCommunication @LauraSicola

_____

_____

_____

124

Who you are talking to, when, where, and why? Answer, then decide the best verbal, vocal, and visual cues to use. #CommandTheRoom @LauraSicola

_____

_____

_____

125

Figure out who your audience
is, and deliver your message in
a way that resonates with them.
#LeadershipCommunication @LauraSicola

126

Know when to switch your speech style
to meet different audiences' needs and
expectations. #PrismaticVoice
@LauraSicola

127

If they'll get distracted by your typical speech style, learn to adjust it to resonate better with the group and be fully heard. #ConnectWithTheAudience @LauraSicola

_____

_____

_____

128

You're not inauthentic if you adapt your
style or presentation to fit the needs and
expectations of a particular audience.
It's both authentic and smart.
#ConnectWithTheAudience @LauraSicola

_____

_____

_____

129

#MonochromaticThinking is telling yourself, "That's not me; this is me." It limits your identity and potential for growth. @LauraSicola

---

130

Break Free from #MonochromaticThinking and acknowledge the broad, beautiful spectrum of your own #PrismaticVoice. @LauraSicola

---

131

You speak differently to your family, colleagues, investors, and friends, but it's all authentically you, right?
#LeadershipVoice @LauraSicola

_____

_____

_____

132

Your #PrismaticVoice has all the style colors of a rainbow. Just choose the color that needs to shine brightest in each situation. @LauraSicola

_____

_____

_____

133

Know which parts of your personality need to shine through in a particular moment. Transmit that in your speech style. #ConnectWithTheAudience @LauraSicola

_____

_____

_____

134

Recognize that different audiences
will appreciate different vocal colors
in your speech wardrobe more than
others. It's okay to adjust accordingly!
#ConnectWithTheAudience @LauraSicola

_____

_____

_____

135

#EffectiveSpeakers recognize which style, quality, or features will have the desired effect on a particular audience. @LauraSicola

---

136

Authenticity is feeling comfortable in your own skin and in your own words. Effective leadership is being able to do that while adjusting your speech style as needed. #LeadershipCommunication @LauraSicola

---

137

Let your identity expand with your opportunities, so your evolving speech repertoire will help extend your power and #Influence. @LauraSicola

_____

_____

_____

138

Communication skills are what ultimately make the difference in how others judge your leadership and the kind of #influence you ultimately have. #ExecutivePresence @LauraSicola

_____

_____

_____

139

If you communicate well and inspire others with your vision, they will propel you to the top. #Leadership #Presence #CloseTheDeal @LauraSicola

_____

_____

_____

140

Be your own greatest masterpiece. Inspire others and be inspired. #LeadershipVoice #CloseTheDeal #ExecutivePresence @LauraSicola

_____

_____

_____

Conclusion

In writing this book for you, I wanted to catalyze massive change. By its design, the unique format of the "AHA" book offers food for thought—bite-sized chunks of ideas and insights. But to go from insights to results, I hope you accepted the challenge I posed to you in the introduction, and did some audio and video recordings as you went along, as suggested. It's the only way to gain the (sometimes painful but always enlightening) objectivity to truly see your own gap between how you want to come across to others and how you actually come across. The smaller the gap, the greater your powers of positive influence.

While I typically do longer-term coaching and large-scale team trainings, there are many people who have reported dramatic changes after simply hearing me speak at an event or after our first session of working together, either of which probably took about as long as it took you to read this book. Here are just a few of their comments:

"I learned how to think and speak more strategically. That was the key."

"After my very first session with Laura, I facilitated a meeting with the senior leadership team. Then afterward, the chair of the session called and he said something was different!"

"My expectations were exceeded; we covered a lot of ground in short time. In addition to helping me develop a voice of authority, I learned the tools necessary to tackle issues that were preventing me from fully speaking up, identified holes in my messaging, and started developing a 'vocal branding' plan. I am now so much more confident and aware of how I sound because of her, and it paid off: I received three offers consecutively over the course of three days!"

"Laura's knowledge of business coupled with her expertise in helping me make my best impression to get what I want was invaluable."

"It was truly a mind-opening and life-changing experience. I will never approach an interview—or my career—in the same way again."

I hope you'll go back again and again to read, record, and reflect on these quotes, and that the experience is equally "mind-opening and life-changing" for you. Then please share your discovery with others and with me as you learn to:

Command the room,
Connect with the audience, and
Close the deal!

Here's to becoming a master of influence,

Laura

About the Author

Dr. Laura Sicola is a professional speaker and leadership communication coach, and the founder of Vocal Impact Productions in Philadelphia, PA. She is known for her coaching and live on-camera trainings that turn C-level executives and other leaders into *master influencers* who get to yes and close the deal.

Her mission is to help people project their best leadership image; create loyal, effective teams; and establish their ideal corporate culture by mastering "The 3 Cs" of Vocal Executive Presence: to Command the room, Connect with the audience, and Close the deal.

Dr. Sicola recognizes that executive presence and strong leadership communication skills are fundamental to success regardless of one's formal role or position. In twenty years of coaching, lecturing, researching, and publishing, she has spoken to audiences in the US, Egypt, Japan, Spain, China, and Germany and has worked with clients and students from around the world. She is a coach for the TED Fellows program and works with clients such as Comcast, Chubb, Wikimedia, Independence Blue Cross, Boston Scientific, the US Department of Commerce, IBM, and Women Against Abuse.

She earned her PhD in educational linguistics from the University of Pennsylvania, where she also was faculty from 2001-2013.

Watch her TED talk: Want to sound like a Leader? Start by saying your name right: http://aha.pub/LauraSicolaTEDtalk.

AHAthat™

AHAthat makes it easy to share, author, and promote content. There are over 40,000 quotes (AHAmessages™) by thought leaders from around the world that you can share in seconds for free.

For those who want to author their own book, we have time-tested proven processes that allow you to write your AHAbook™ of 140 digestible, bite-sized morsels in eight hours or less. Once your content is on AHAthat, you have a customized link that you can use to have your fans/advocates share your content and help grow your network.

➲ Start sharing: http://AHAthat.com

➲ Start authoring: http://AHAthat.com/Author

Hey,
Did You
AHAthat™?

Laura Sicola
AHAthat Author

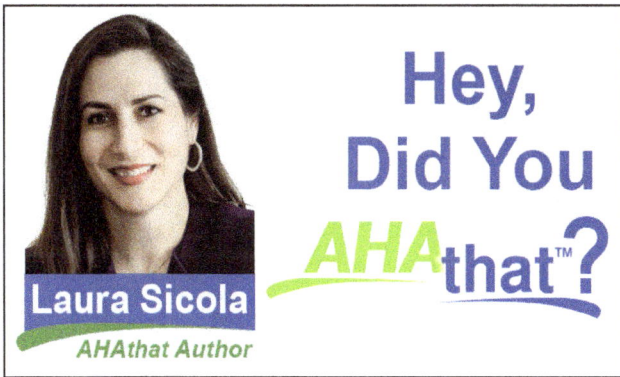

Please go directly to this book in AHAthat and share each AHAmessage socially at
http://aha.pub/LeadershipInfluence

www.ingramcontent.com/pod-product-compliance
Lightning Source LLC
Chambersburg PA
CBHW071159200326
41519CB00018B/5281